COMBAT
JIU-JITSU

By Norman Leff

First published in 2001 by
CFW Enterprises, Inc.

Copyright © 2001 by
Unique Publications, Inc.

Disclaimer

ISBN: 0-86568-190-2
Library of Congress Catalog Number: 2001-131619

Distributed by:
Unique Publications
4201 Vanowen Place
Burbank, CA 91505
(800) 332-3330

First edition
05 04 03 02 01 00 99 98 97 1 3 5 7 9 10 8 6 4 2

Printed in the United States of America

Editor: John Steven Soet
Design: George Foon
Cover: George Chen

Dedication

*I would like to dedicate this book to my wife
Rosita, a former folkloric dancer and instructor.*

Table of Contents

Acknowledgements

Without the encouragement of John Steven Soet and C.F.W. Enterprises this book could not have been written. I dedicate this book to the ancient masters of Jiu Jitsu and especially to the instructors who influenced my life in the martial arts:

* To **Tanaka Sensei** who taught me what combat Jiu Jitsu was all about.

* To **Shihan Michael De Pasquale, Sr.** who revealed to me many of the ancient secrets of Jiu Jitsu.

* To **Judo Gene LeBell** whose concepts, ideas, techniques and traning methods that I adopted.

* To **Sifu Tang** whose instruction and knowledge of Chinese Boxing and Chin Na made me into a better martial artist.

* To **Professor Lee** who taught me how powerful the art of Korean Hapkido can be.

* To **Homura Sensei** who instructed me the art of combat karate. Whose teachings made me appreciate how devastating karate can be as a self-defense art.

* Last but not least to my long friend **Roget Kervabon** who I have not seen in over 30 years. Whose friendship and personal kindness I will never forget.

A typical judo class in 1960, Norm (top left).

Scenes from Norm's dojo
(circa 1980) in Tujunga, Calif.

The dojo was called
"Yoshitsune" – dojo
of a Samurai.

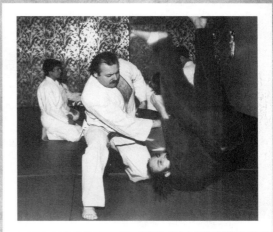

Norm taught as he
was taught, which
meant a high turnover.

At his prime fighting weight of 250 lbs.,
he was known as "The Clark Gable of the martial arts."

Mr. Olympia, Samir Bannout

Oleg Taktarov

Mark Kerr (left) and Frank Shamrock (right)

**"The Armenian Assassin"
Gokor Chivichyan**

Dan Severn

Introduction

It was like another world when I began to study Jiu-Jitsu at the age of nine years old. At that time the United States was at war with Germany, Italy and Japan. Much has changed since that time, and I along with it. During that period most Americans had heard of a strange and mystical Japanese fighting style call "Judo" and it was considered the ultimate self-defense art. They equated Judo black belts with superhuman beings. They were the fastest guns in the west and the toughest guys in town. So if one wanted to study the art of self-defense during that time one would either study Judo or Jiu-Jitsu. (Note: Judo was supposed to be the modern version of Jiu-Jitsu at that period. One's choices were very limited.)

"They equated Judo black belts with superhuman beings."

Today there are so many different martial arts to choose from that it becomes difficult for a beginner to decide the right martial art for his particular needs. It must be very confusing for an individual to know what is the right martial art to study.

When I first began studying Jiu-Jitsu I was only interested in learning how to defend myself. My interest at the present time, more than 50 years later, remains the same. I can truthfully state that I still consider myself a self-defense student. Perhaps I am an advanced student but, nevertheless, still a student who continues to learn more about this craft.

Many people have asked me why I decided to study Jiu-Jitsu. The answer to this question is very simple. Japanese Jiu-Jitsu was the fighting art of the Samurai. Jiu-Jitsu (also spelled Ju Jutsu or Ju Jitsu) developed its fighting techniques on the battlefields of Asia. The essence and core of this art is in its self-defense techniques. It is one of the few martial arts that primarily are dedicated to armed and unarmed combat. However, I have studied many different styles of Japanese, Chinese, Korean and Western self-defense arts during my long career.

I first studied Karate-do in 1960. The instructors usually did not teach self-defense in the classes. The classes consisted of lots of exercises, basic techniques, kata, one-step, two-step, three-step kumite and kumite itself. I would beg my instructors to teach me different techniques of unarmed hand to hand combat. The majority of them were sympathetic to my request. They generally taught me what I wanted to know. They did it most of the time, but not all of the time. Their reasons for not teaching self-defense was that karate in itself was based on self-defense. Therefore, it became superfluous.

When I competed in Judo I encountered the same problem. I had to beseech my instructors to teach me techniques of personal defense. When I began to study competition Judo I did not realize that the self-defense aspect of Judo would be eliminated. I always thought that Judo was an art of self-defense. I was completely ignorant and unaware that Judo was also a sport.

One of the main reasons that I studied Judo was because of its combative hand to hand combat techniques. It is this author's opinion that combat Judo is still one of the most effective systems in unarmed hand to hand combat. Another system that impressed me was the Russian art of Sambo (a form of Russian Jiu-Jitsu.)

In 1954 I met a former Soviet Army Officer who had escaped from the old Soviet Union during the second world war. He taught me Russian self-defense: Sambo. My Russian friend was very skillful at it. He had extraordinary ability in hand to hand combat. During my martial arts career I have had many different teachers. Many were professional instructors in the martial arts. There were others who did not teach for money, but were nevertheless fantastic martial artists.

"Japanese Jiu-Jitsu was the fighting art of the Samurai."

There was a special sensei of mine that I met when I lived in South America. He made a tremendous impact on me that has lasted up to this time. Tanaka sensei taught me the art of Kempo Jiu-Jitsu. More will be said of Tanaka sensei in other parts of this book.

Another inspiring sensei of mine is Grandmaster Michael De Pasquale, Senior, a man of great martial arts skills and knowledge. Besides being a fantastic Jiu-Jitsuka he is also a man of culture and breeding. De Pasquale sensei taught me a very aggressive and combative Jiu-Jitsu. In this book I will share some of the secretive techniques of combat Jiu-Jitsu. Combat Jiu-Jitsu is one of the most devastating arts of self-defense in the history of the world.

What is Combat Jiu-Jitsu?

As I mentioned in the introduction, I have been training in martial arts for over 50 years, primarily in Jiu-Jitsu. Combat Jiu-Jitsu is the result of that half century of experience. But to understand the essence of Combat Jiu-Jitsu, the reader must first become familiar with its roots.

CLASSICAL JIU-JITSU

Jiu-Jitsu is the ancient Japanese martial art of armed and unarmed combat. It is the mother of all Japanese modern Budo arts. Judo, Aikido, Shorinji Kempo, Wado Ryu Karate-Do, Korean Hapkido, etc. were founded by Jiu-Jitsu men. One could fill a book with the names of the great masters of the martial arts who had studied Jiu-Jitsu.

Jiu-Jitsu is still practiced in Japan as a secretive martial art, and the Japanese masters of this art are not interested in sharing its secrets with other martial arts systems. Authentic Samurai Jiu-Jitsu techniques are closely guarded by the guardians of the various styles of Jiu-Jitsu that have survived in Japan up to the present time. As a matter of fact, there are very few books on authentic Jiu-Jitsu that one can purchase in any book store. There are many books on Karate, Aikido, Taekwondo, Hapkido, Judo and different styles of Chinese boxing. Classical texts have been published in Japan on the various styles of Karate, Aikido and Judo by the founders of these arts. Not one classical text on Japanese Jiu-Jitsu has ever been published on Jiu-Jitsu in the United States.

Much of the Japanese public is ignorant about this art. The most popular style of Jiu-Jitsu in Japan today is Brazilian Jiu-Jitsu, which derived from a style of several combined Jiu-Jitsu disciplines taught by Jigoro Kano, founder of Judo. Although Brazilian Jiu-Jitsu is a proven and highly effective fighting art, the curriculum lacks many of the more advanced techniques taught in classical Japanese Jiu-Jitsu. Foremost among these lacking elements is the study of atemi waza.

ATEMI WAZA

The atemi waza is a secretive and devastating art. Its secrets are closely guarded by all the leading masters of Combat Jiu-Jitsu. Many of the atemi strikes are definitely related to the sword techniques of the samurai. An example of this is the Tegatana (sword hand) technique. Others are obviously from the art of Kempo (Chinese boxing).

It is said that a Chinese man by the name of Chen Yuan Pin, also known by other names, introduced a fighting art that resembled Pugilism and it was incorporated into the schools (ryu) of Jiu-Jitsu. Chen Yuan Pin's teaching of Kempo is uncertain. It is reported variously as 1627, 1644, 1648 and 1650. His exact profession is largely unknown. Some historians say he was a craftsman, poet, diplomat, fighting monk, etc. Much of the information we have about him is open to pure speculation, but what is certain is the definite influence Kempo (Chinese boxing) had on Jiu-Jitsu.

The Japanese martial art masters of Jiu-Jitsu were not so naive or arrogant as to believe that their system of fighting could not be improved by adopting the fighting techniques of Chinese boxing. Many of the Japanese martial art teachers were also military men. At that period of time Japan was a militaristic nation that was constantly engaged in warfare in Asia. They occupied Korea, and various parts of China. The Chinese masters of the various style of Chinese boxing instructed the Japanese military in their secretive fighting arts.

Legend says that a Jiu-Jitsu master named Okayama Hochiroji, a wandering teacher, was once engaged in a battle with a hundred laborers. He and some assistants were said to have easily put them to flight. It was he who evolved the art of the atemi. There is another interesting report of an extraordinary Jiu-Jitsu man named Shisero Sasagawa who is said to have knocked out a charging bull with a single blow. One hundred years ago later this feat was accomplished by the late great karate-ka Mas Oyama, founder of Kyokushin Karate-do. Mas Oyama had studied the Kempo techniques of Korean and Chinese boxing.

"The most popular style of Jiu–Jitsu in Japan today is Brazilian Jiu–Jitsu."

An article in a well-known martial arts magazine some years ago featured the late founder of Shotokan Karate, Master Gichin Funakoshi. One of his students was Hironori Otsuka who became a master of Yoshih Ryu Jiu-Jitsu at the age of 29. Otsuka explained that when Funakoshi arrived in Japan he was amazed at the similarity between his Karate and the Atemi found in Jiu-Jitsu. In fact, he was astonished when he saw Otsuka demonstrate atemi, and was sure he must have been practicing karate. Master Otsuka later became the founder of Wado Ryu Karate-do.

Evolution of Jiu-Jitsu

To understand Jiu-Jitsu you have to understand its strategy, tactics and concepts. You also have to understand the historical times of the samurai. At one time Jiu-Jitsu had more than 700 different schools (Ryu). Different styles had different strategies, tactics and techniques. This art can be described as a total martial art.

Japanese Jiu-Jitsu is a complete fighting art, and it has nothing to do with the sporting aspects of competition and contests. All martial art systems must have a wide variety of techniques in order to be effective. No student can excel in every phase of the martial arts. Some students are better in kicking while others are better with their hands. Some prefer hand and foot fighting techniques. For these reasons, the style must have something for everyone and it ought to be tailored to fit the individual student's talents and needs. In this manner the student can choose his or her needs and not be left out.

Different styles specialized in immobilization techniques. Still others concentrated on percussion techniques, etc. Japanese Jiu-Jitsu had a vast array of throwing, ground fighting, strangling, immobilization techniques, etc. Each school would usually specialize in various techniques to their respective needs.

For example, since the samurai had weapons, the counterattack against them consisted of seizing their wrists to prevent them form pulling out their weapons. This strategy was used in unarmed combat. Once the wrist was seized the counter attack was to immobilize the arm by using a joint lock. If the samurai wore armor then kicking and striking might not prevent him from pulling out his or using his weapon. Nevertheless, there were some styles of Jiu-Jitsu that primarily used Kempo techniques against their enemies. Kempo and Hakuda specialty is to kick, strike, thrust, poke, stab, punch, etc.

Combat Jiu-Jitsu is an art that is so flexible and it has such a vast number of techniques to choose from that the Jiu-Jitsuka can cope with everything from an annoying attack to a deadly one. This book will focus on combative techniques that are taken from the various different styles of Jiu-Jitsu rather than concentrating on a particular style.

THE ABC'S OF COMBAT JIU-JITSU

The techniques of Combat Jiu-Jitsu include: throws, takedowns, choking, grappling, joint locks of the entire body. Very painful torsions are done on the arms, legs, neck, back, wrists, shoulders, etc. Special methods of strangling are applied on the opponent that are extremely dangerous. Combat Jiu-Jitsu uses heavy impact throwing techniques that will quickly end any physical confrontation that one has in a fight. If the throw is done correctly it will seriously injure or knock out the enemy.

Ground grappling is an integral part of Combat Jiu-Jitsu. However, ground grappling is not practiced as a sport, and all of its techniques are for self-defenses purposes.

The most devastating aspect of Combat Jiu-Jitsu is the study of the atemi waza. This is especially true in the art of Kempo Jiu-Jitsu. The advanced students of Combat Jiu-Jitsu are experts in the art of attacking the vital spots of the human body with one's natural weapons. The students are taught special methods of hitting, kicking, striking, punching, thrusting, poking, jabbing, ripping, kneeing, etc. One learns how to forge every part of one's body as a natural weapon. The techniques of the atemi waza include the study of the vital or weak points (kyusho) of the human anatomy. The students learn these anatomical points of weakness, and then they learn the methods of attacking them.

Precautionary advice is given to all disciples of Combat Jiu-Jitsu if they were engaged in combat fighting:

1) Calmly survey the conditions of the opponent.

2) Quick judgment and speedy action are essential for the purpose of forestalling the opponent.

3) According to circumstances, the atemi is preferable to throwing techniques (Nagewaza) especially when you are confronted by a number of antagonists.

4) Notice whether your antagonist is armed or not.

5) You may assist your art by briskly shouting at an opponent.

6) When you are suddenly placed in a dangerous position, you must determine to fall with your enemy (take him down with you in a "sacrifice" throw).

7) Don't be off your guard after you have obtained victory.

In real circumstances being off your guard constitutes your greatest enem. When you travel in dangerous places, you must be careful in every respect. Whether your enemy is armed or not or whether he intends to fall upon you suddenly, will all be clearly known to you if you are very attentive. Although this precautionary advice was given a very long time ago much of it still can be applied to modern times.

What has changed since the time of the samurai is technology, not human nature. We live in the age of science, man has walked on the moon and he achieved fantastic scientific breakthroughs, but his basic nature has not changed. Man is the ultimate predator. Human beings are the most dangerous species on this planet.

We can delude ourselves in believing that all people are good and compassionate. One only has to read the newspapers to understand how bad some people can be. There are those who will not hesitate to commit heinous acts of violence against law abiding citizens. There have been so many innocent victims that have been raped, assaulted, robbed, murdered, crippled, beaten by these sadistic human monsters. So many lives have been smashed, torn apart and cut short by these evil criminals.

Learning the art of self-defense should be as important as learning how to read and write. It should be part of everyone's education in today's world. Every one of us is vulnerable in becoming a victim of these nefarious individuals. Instruction in Combat Jiu-Jitsu is like buying life insurance. It is a must because all of us need it. The fighting techniques in this book have existed for centuries and I have not invented any new combative techniques. They have been tested in warfare and in personal encounters.

However, for them to work they require effort, consistency, discipline, endless amount repetitions, practice, fanatical determination, patience and perseverance etc. The more you practice the better you will become. Bear in mind the criminal and the bully want a sheep as a victim.

The bully wants to browbeat and intimate his victim. The criminal and bully are not interested in confronting a vicious tiger. So be a tiger or a small tiger, but a tiger nevertheless.

A NOTE ABOUT CONDITIONING

Due to lack of space I did not include a chapter on exercise. I felt that the readers would be better served if I dedicated this book to Combat Jiu-Jitsu techniques. Nevertheless, physical fitness should be a part of everyone's daily schedule. Your body is the house you live in therefore, take care of it and it will pay you dividends in good health. When constructing an exercise program be sure to diversify it. Your exercise program should include exercises for strength, cardiovascular fitness and exercises for flexibility.

Do exercises for your entire body. Never stretch cold muscles. Make certain that you warm up before stretching. There are certain stretching exercises that can aggravate certain lower back problems. I am a great advocate of weight training. However, when lifting weights, be careful not to lift too heavily. Keep in mind that weight training done improperly can cause severe chronic injuries.

Do lots of pull ups, dips and push-ups for upper body strength. Include a variety of abdominal and neck exercises to strengthen those areas. Do some exercises everyday. All of us should devote at least an hour a day in exercising. Many people make excuses for not working out. The most common one is lack of time. My advice to you is to make the time! The late legendary Karate master Mas Oyama said: "Train more than you sleep".

Remember being in good physical condition may save life in a street attack. Do not forget to make exercise part of your daily routine.

Chapter One

The Atemi Waza

THE ATEMI WAZA

The application of practical and realistic techniques of the Atemi is based on knowledge of the vital points of the human body. The exponent of this art never uses any techniques that are complex or complicated. His strategy is simple: eliminate the attacker, and his ability to attack or retaliate. This is done in a rapid and efficient manner. The student of this art tries to overcome his adversary by diplomacy and guile if he can. However, if he must, he uses ruthless and savage techniques in order to survive.

THE MERIDIAN CHANNELS

The Meridian Channels are: liver, lungs, large intestines, stomach, spleen, heart, small intestines, bladder, kidneys, pericardium, and three heater. Attacking the meridian channels can bring about organ dysfunction. The circulatory and respiratory systems will be affected. Violent strikes will rupture arteries and induce internal bleeding. This type of trauma will lead to death if the victim does not receive medical attention immediately.

However, certain powerful and forceful strikes can kill the victim instantly. Attacking the circulatory pathways that lead to the vital organs is a very complex type of art that genuine masters of Jiu-Jitsu and Kempo use. It is a very esoteric and secretive art that is closely guarded by its guardian as it should be. It is the Japanese version of the deadly Chinese art of Dim Mak.

The Atemi Strikes

Ready position

Hammer fist to the crown of the head

Ready position

Sword-hand strike to temple

Ready position

Groin slap or pull (attack to groin)

Ready position

Sword strike to collar bone

Ready position

Uppercut punch to solar plexus

Knee strike

To the face or head

Ready position

Wrist grab

Wrist lock

Ready position

Strike to elbow joint

**Arm bar across shoulder and
elbow strike to ribs**

Ready position

Wrist grab

Stepping back kick

to inside of thigh

Rear Atemi

Ready position

Palm thrust to the head

Ready position

Punch to kidney

Ready position

Thrust kick to back of knee

Ready position

Reverse punch

To lower back

Ready position

Straight vertical punch to middle of back

Ready position

Various groin attacks

Ready position

Pull Uke back

Downward elbow strike to chest

Ready position

Sword strike to nape of neck

Ready position

Seize wrist

Strike arm

Ready position

Cross wrist grab

Uke hook punches with his left, which is blocked

Downward strike to elbow joint

Ready position

Double wrist grab

Head butt

Chapter Two
Locks, Throws and Control Techniques

Jiu-Jitsu has a vast amount of different locks, throws, chokes and immobilization techniques than any other martial art. In this chapter we will focus on some of these techniques which will help the reader in controlling and immobilizing a dangerous antagonist.

Grappling on the ground in a street altercation is simply a bad strategy for obvious reasons. It places one in a vulnerable position and the disadvantages outweigh the advantages. If the assailant has friends and you take him down, and start to grapple with him on the ground with submission holds you can be hit, kicked and stomped from behind or the side. It is a bad fight plan! Avoid fighting on the ground at all costs in the street.

However, if one is taken off his feet one must be able to grapple effectively and brutally for self-defense purposes. One must be able to use Atemi and pressure point fighting techniques. Try to get to your feet as soon as possible because fighting on the ground is fraught with danger. I know that this sounds like a paradox. A Jiu-Jitsuka is a complete fighter and he should know how to grapple on the ground for self-defense.

Therefore, if one is in an area where no one is around then ground fighting is permissable. As long as you do not endanger your well being or your ability to survive. **Bear in mind that grappling for self-defense is completely different from sport grappling.** It is like comparing night to day or apples to oranges. The reality in grappling for self-defense is that you are grappling inorder to save one's life.

Against a Kick

Uke (black gi) and Tori (white gi) square off

As Uke kicks, Tori sidesteps
out of the way

Catching the kick

And striking the leg

And following up with a strike
to the face

Against a Bear Hug

Tori is in a bear hug with his arms pinned

He twists out through opening before Uke locks

Tori spreads both of his arms with aiki energy

Tori does not allow Uke to lock in and also strikes Uke with an atemi

Delivers a groin strike

Arm locks him downward

And finishes him with a knee to the face

Against a Rush

Uke and Tori face off

As Uke begins to move, Tori strikes to the wrist

Brings his arm up in a wrist flex

Levers him down

And applies his control – armlock over lower leg

Attacking with a Cross Wrist Lock

Uke and Tori face off

Before Uke can react, Tori reaches across with his left hand and grabs Uke's left wrist

He quickly pulls Uke's wrist up to his right shoulder and wraps his right hand around the back of Uke's arm.

He presses down with both his arms and his shoulders

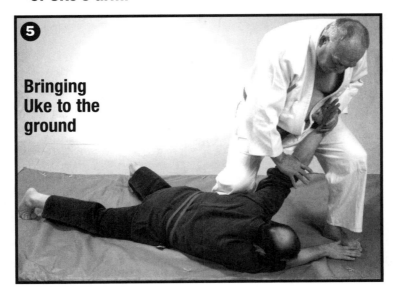

Bringing Uke to the ground

Attacking with a Same-Hand Wrist Lock

Uke and Tori face off

Tori grabs Uke's right hand with his left

He pulls Uke's arm out and steps in with his whole body, to his right, holding Uke's wrist with both hands

He flips his body to the right

Bringing Uke to the ground

Attacking with a Hammerlock

Uke and Tori face off

Tori grabs Uke's right wrist (inside) with his right hand

He then takes control by grabbing the wrist with both hands

And steps behind Uke, twisting up in a hammer lock

Attacking with Arm Bar Choke

Uke and Tori face off

Tori grabs back of Uke's gi

He steps forward as he
pulls on Uke's gi

And places his left forearm
against Uke's throat

Attacking from Behind

Tori is behind Uke

He steps forward and wraps his right arm around Uke's neck

He places his left hand on Uke's shoulder and steps in

By pulling back with even a slight pressure

He off-balances Uke

And brings him to the mat

Please be careful with this devastating technique!

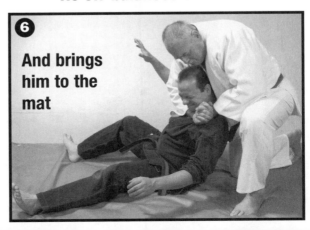

Sweep from the Front

Uke and Tori face off

Tori steps in and grabs Uke's right hand

While pressing his middle knuckle to the notch of the throat

He then steps forward and reaches around Uke's right leg with his left leg

And sweeps him to the mat

He maintains his hold on the wrist

Which enables him to administer more punishment if more force is necessary to end the confrontation

Rear Choke

Tori is behind Uke

He steps in and wraps his right arm in a "V" around Uke's neck (note, not the throat, the sides of the neck)

He slips his left hand

Behind Uke's head

Which enables him to apply pressure to the carotid

Shoulder Throw

Uke and Tori face off

**Tori steps in and grabs
Uke's right wrist with
both hands**

**Steps around with his
right foot as he raises
Uke's arm up**

Pivots around quickly

**And throws Uke
over his shoulder**

Hip Throw

① Uke and Tori face off

② Uke grabs Tori by the collar

③ Tori grabs Uke's right sleeve with his left hand while wrapping his right arm around Uke's back

④ Tori begins to pivot

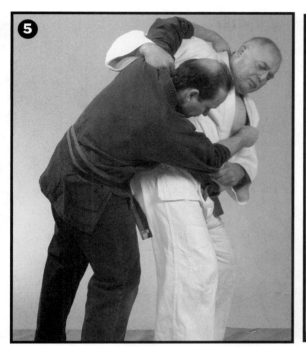

Throwing Uke over his hip

To the ground

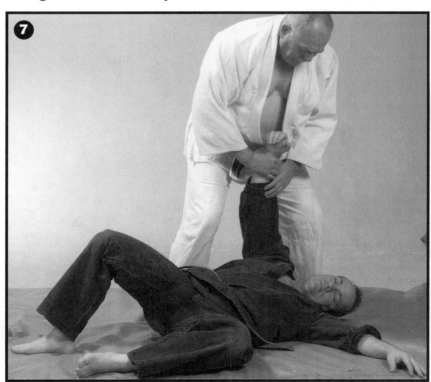

Where he can apply a wrist lock

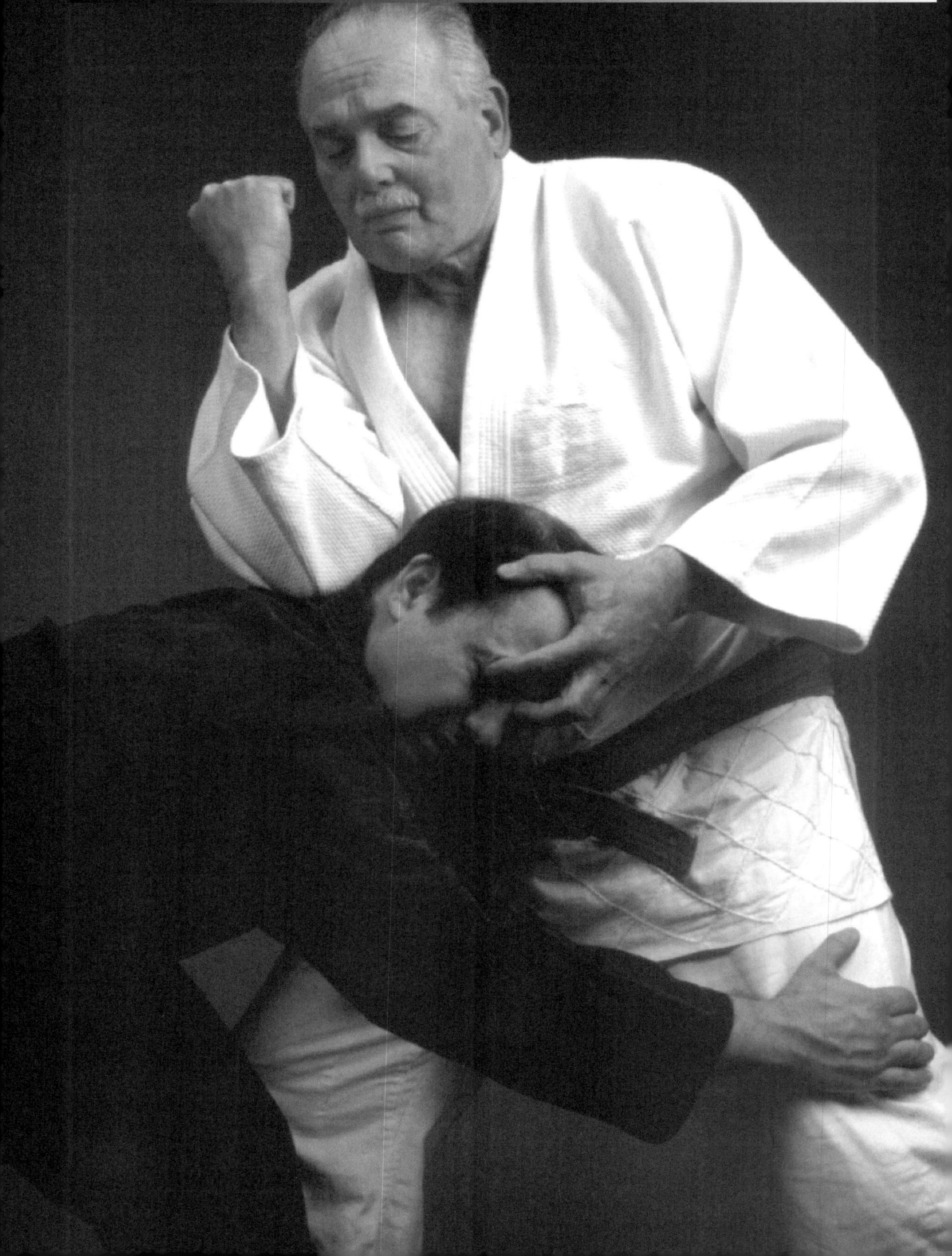

Chapter Three
Counterattack

Whether the assailant seizes, grabs, chokes, kicks, or punches the defender, he must react automatically, effectively, and explosively to end the fight rapidly. The defender may have to respond in a violent and savage way if the attack is deadly. If the attack is not deadly or threatening then the response must be different. There are a vast amount of techniques to choose from if the attack is more of a pushing, seizing or slapping one. It will also depend how dangerous, athletic and skillful the attacker is. If he knows how to fight then the situation becomes more complicated and uncertain for the defender. Also his physical size becomes important. Is the attacker a large, medium or small individual? Is he muscular? Is he under the influence of alcohol or drugs? Is he in an enraged or hysterical state of mind?

There are too many unknown factors to consider. When one is attacked , one has no time to think and contemplate the attacker. One's reaction must be swift in order to save one's well being. It is hard to look into the mind of another person and know his intentions. If one's judgment is poor one can end up in a hospital or in the morgue. However, we all must think of the legal consequences. If one reacts too harshly the one can be arrested. This can lead to a lot of legal problems such as a civil suit, incarceration (jail time) etc.

Spending time in jail is not a pretty picture to contemplate and experience. One can be convicted on a felony charge that will haunt the defender for the rest of his life.

It will also cost the defender an enormous amount of money on legal fees. If one does not have money for a private attorney then one will suffer the consequences. It is a no win situation. The problem is that one may feel justified in defending oneself, but the police, district attorney and court may feel differently.

Remember, martial artists have been stereotyped by movies as something more than they are. As a result, a martial artist is usually punished by the courts in a phys-ical alteration unless he can prove beyond a shadow of a doubt that he had no choice. However, if the defender has a great deal of money and he can hire a expensive lawyer then he has a better chance to be exonerated. The poor man has little chance of finding justice in our present judicial system. I am not saying it is not possible, but it is like playing against a man who has loaded dice. Do your best to avoid problems, espe-cially physical problems, with people. Two minutes of uncontrolled anger can ruin your life and cause your loved ones heartaches and lots of grief.

"Think and meditate on these words."

Regardless, the fact remains that there are times when one has no other choice but to save oneself from a sav-age beating. The best advice that was given to me by my instructors was to end the fight as quickly as possible in a humane way. Never ever use more force than is neces-sary. Neutralize the attacker's ability to hurt you (render him impotent). That is the key to survival! Think and meditate on these words.

Strategy & Tactics

1. Break all holds from the beginning or onset. Do not allow the assailant to lock in because if he does it will become more difficult to break the hold.

2. Use the Atemi to nullify his attack.

3. There will be times when one can use a pressure point attack to release the hold.

4. Keep your antagonist off balance both physically and mentally.

5. Attack the vital spots of the body if the attacker is very dangerous.

6. Move out of the way from punches, kicks and seizures.

7. Fight your attacker on his blind side.

8. Use soft blocks against hard punches and kicks.

Try to redirect his attack away from yourself. If you can run away from a fight then do so. Do not think of it as cowardice or lacking in courage. I think of it as being smart and having good sense. Generally speaking it will be an encounter with a stranger -- person whom you will probably never see again in your life. It is not worthwhile to get involved in a brawl that no one can predict the outcome. It can have horrible consequences either for him or the defender. If you are attacked you have no choice but to defend yourself, and your well being in a sensible and responsible manner.

Against a Double Lapel Seizure

Uke and Tori face off

Uke grabs Tori by the lapels

Tori steps in and delivers an underhand atemi to
the solar plexus while grasping Uke's wrist

He then grabs both of Uke's wrists and levers his hands back

And delivers a kick to the groin or midsection

Against a Single Lapel Seizure

Uke and Tori face off

**Uke grabs Tori's lapel
with his left hand**

Tori quickly grabs Uke's wrist

**Tori grabs Uke's left wrist with his
right hand and palm strikes Uke's
right shoulder with his left hand. This
prevents Uke from punching Tori.**

**Tori twists Uke around
and throws him**

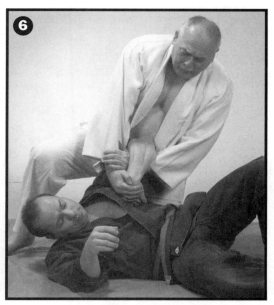

To the ground

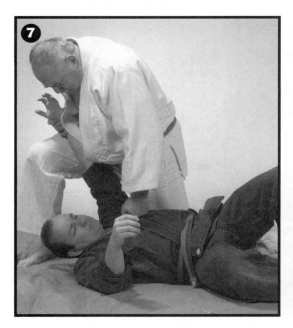

Tori follows up with an atemi

And an elbow and wrist lock

Against a Cross Wrist Grab

Uke and Tori face off

Uke cross-grabs Tori's wrist

Tori quickly twists his wrist upward

and applies an arm bar pin

Tori strikes the elbow joint

Tori applies an aiki arm bar.

Against a Headlock

Uke and Tori face off

Uke grabs Tori around the neck with his left arm

As Uke applies a headlock,

Tori applies a nerve pinch

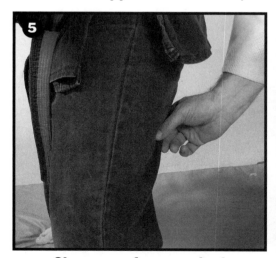

Close-up of nerve pinch

Tori then pushes forward on Uke's arms

Steps back while grabbing the hand with his left hand

And presses on the elbow with his right

He then applies a wrist lock

And turns his body to the right

Bringing Uke to the mat

Where he can administer further punishment if this does not end the confrontation

Against a Tackle

Tori faces Uke

Uke rushes in

And wraps his arms around Tori

And attempts to tackle him

Tori strikes to the ears

Taking him down in a twisting neck lock (Be Careful)!

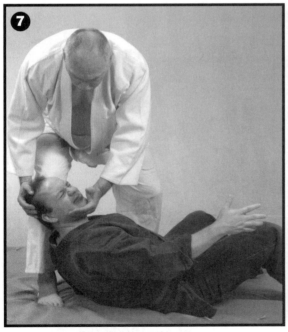

Tori places his right hand

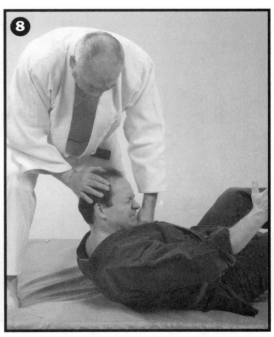

Behind Uke's head and his left hand on his chest

Against a Front Kick

Uke and Tori face off

Uke attacks with a front kick

Tori scoop blocks it

Locking Uke's leg

Tori twists to his left

And throws Uke down

Then presses down on the foot with the weight of his body to lock the leg

Against a Front Strangle

Tori and Uke face off

Uke seizes Tori's throat

Tori responds with
an atemi strike

And throws him with a
double armlock throw

By pulling Uke's left hand under his right arm

And twisting

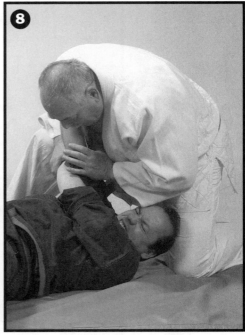

To bring him down

On the ground, he applies a finishing hold

Against a "Sucker Punch"

Uke and Tori face each other

Uke throws a punch, Tori parries with his right hand

Tori intercepts the punch under his right arm and grabs the wrist

He takes him down

With a straight arm bar

Arm bar across the chest
(All locks should be practiced carefully)

Against Mount Position

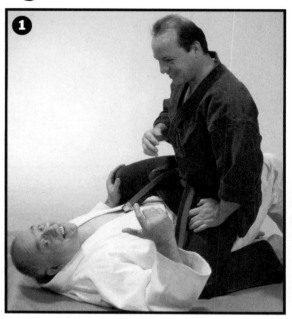

Uke is on top of Tori in a mount position

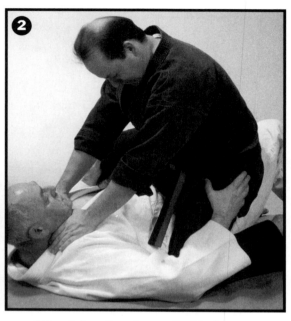

Uke tries to strangle Tori with both hands

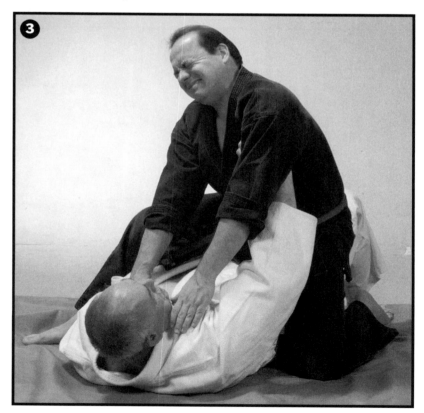

Tori twists Uke's pectoral muscle violently and painfully

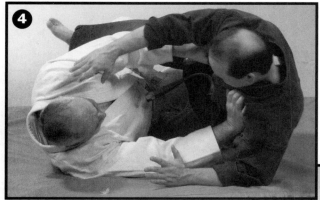

Breaking the hold

**Tori throws
Uke to the side**

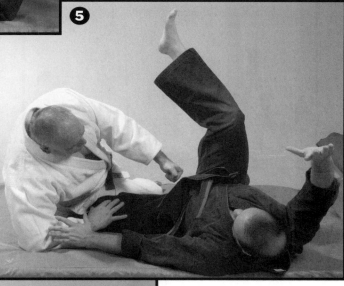

**And
strikes
him in the
groin**

Against Ground Choke

Uke has Tori on the ground
and is choking him

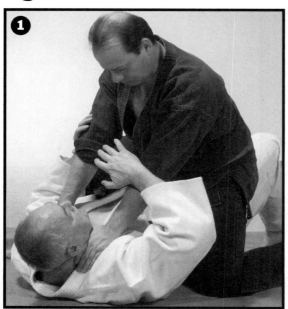

Tori pushes on Uke's elbow joing
to weaken the choke

Tori strike's Uke's neck with sword hand

He follows up with an arm bar

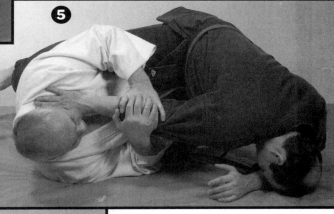

Tori then places his left leg over Uke's right arm

And under his chin and applies an armlock

Against a Ground Punch

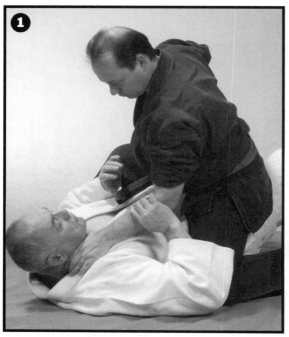

Uke seizes Tori's throat
and attempts

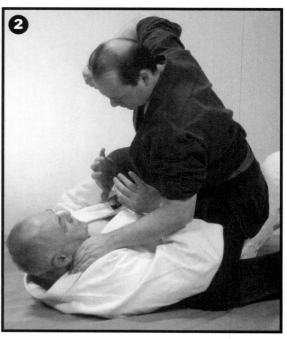

To punch him with his right hand

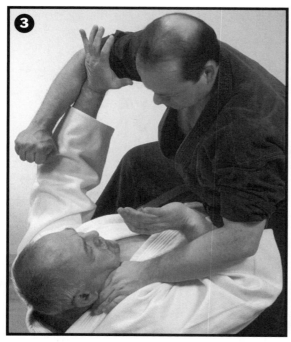

Tori catch blocks the punch
with his left hand

And strikes Uke with an atemi

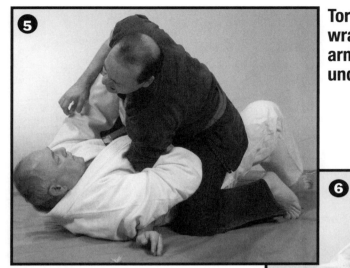

Tori then wraps his right arm over and under Uke's

Left arm and secures an elbow lock

He then throws Uke to his right side and breaks his arm

Against a Strangle Hold

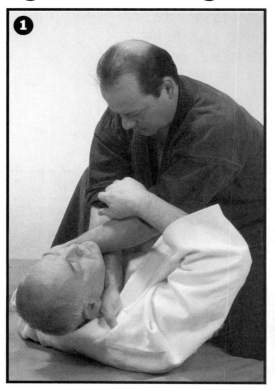

Uke is trying to strangle Tori

Tori jabs his fingers into Uke's suprasternal notch

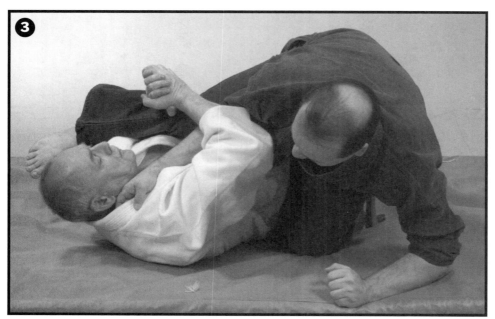

And hooks Uke's leg and twists to his right

**Locking up
Uke's leg**

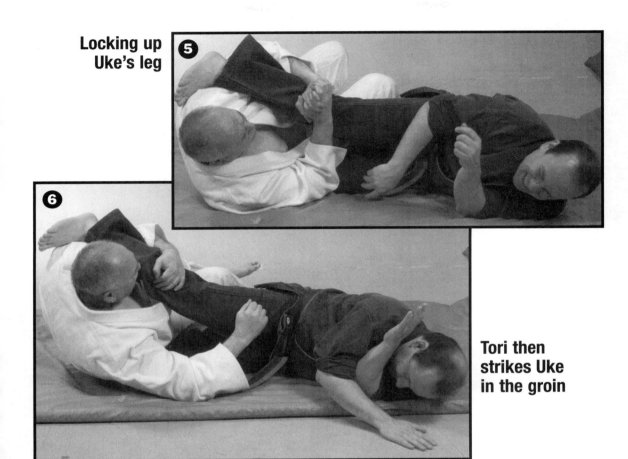

**Tori then
strikes Uke
in the groin**

**And secures
an ankle
lock on Uke**

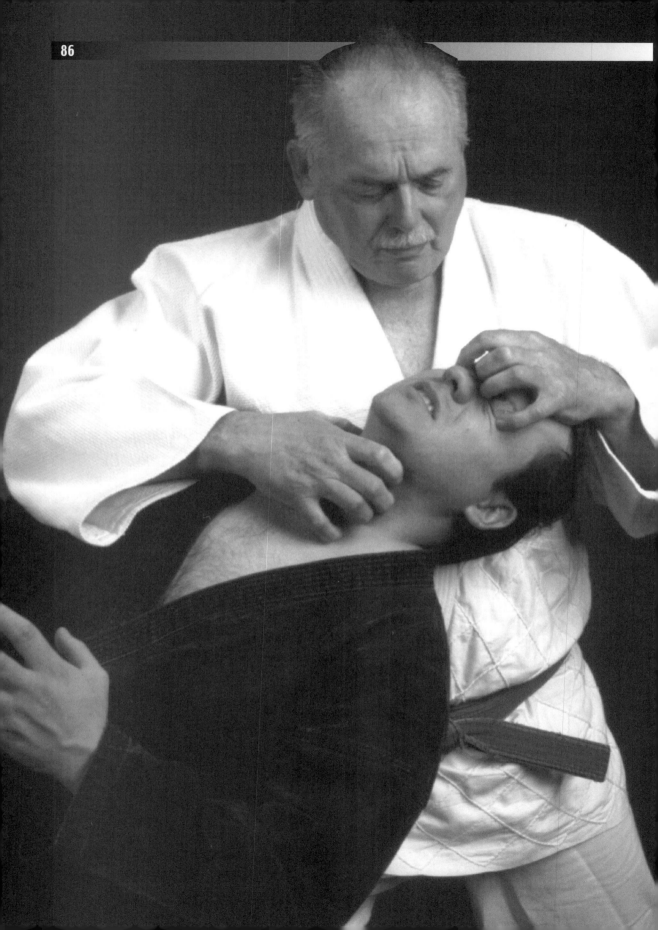

Chapter Four

Fight Stoppers

The ability to end the fight before it begins is an art in itself. They say that the best defense is a good offense. This is the ultimate technique in the martial arts; to be able to stop the attacker before he can hurt the defender. Legend says that all great masters of the martial arts had this ability. It was as if they could read their adversaries' minds. Was it some inmate psychic ability that these masters possessed? Did they practice or know some form of mental telepathy that gave them this skill or was their intuition or insight abnormally developed? Perhaps they know some secretive esoteric methods that they did not divulge to the majority of their disciples. This author believes that there are still some masters who have these uncanny ability and skills. These are interesting questions to reflect and ponder upon.

"This is the ultimate technique in the martial arts."

Nevertheless, there are techniques and tactics that can give one an edge in a fight. It takes intensive training, practice and patience to acquire them. It can be obtained if one has enough dedication and dogged perseverance. I would be less than candid with the readers of this book to tell you that it comes easy. There is no free lunch and there has never been something for nothing. It takes untiring and endless practice to be a good combat man. If you are willing to pay the price then you will achieve success in Combat Jiu-Jitsu.

"There is no free lunch and there has never been something for nothing."

However, the key to success is hard work and tenacious effort. The techniques in this chapter will allow you to gain some advantages over your assailants if you follow the strategy, and tactics to the letter. Follow the concepts and do not forget to practice, practice, practice and practice some more.

Against a Straight Punch

Tori and Uke face off

Uke attempts a left punch

Tori blocks Uke's blow with his left
and strikes with an atemi

Tori seizes Uke's left wrist
with his hand

He then takes Uke down
on his chest

Twisting on Uke's wrist

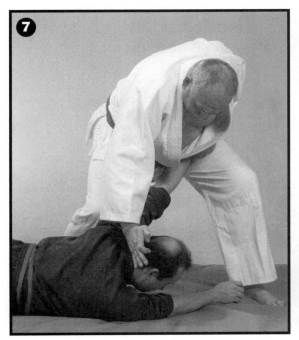

Tori then strikes Uke on the nape of
the neck with a sword hand strike

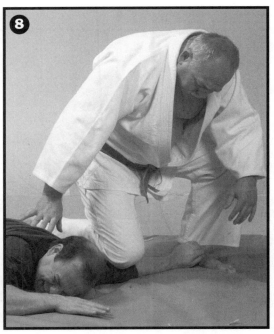

And pins him to the ground
with his knee

Against a Left Hook

Tori and Uke face off

Uke strikes Tori with his left punch. Tori parries the strike with a right, deflecting parry while chambering his kick

Tori delivers a full force downward kick to Uke's knee

Taking him to the ground

Tori then chambers

And finishes Uke with a stomp kick to the lower abdomen

Against a Right Cross

Tori and Uke face off

Tori sidesteps Uke's right punch

And deflects to the right

He then kicks Uke while grasping
Uke's right wrist

The kick strikes the rib cage
as Tori pulls

And he steps back and to the side
to apply an arm bar

He cranks the arm bar

Finishing his assailant

Beating Him to the Punch

Uke menaces Tori with words and threatens to attack him

Applying the old saying, "The best defense is an offense," Tori rushes in and grabs Uke's right arm under his left while applying an atemi strike to the face

He then pulls back on Uke's right arm while pressing down on his face

Taking him to the ground

And pinning him with his knee

Against a "Sucker Punch"

Uke and Tori face each other

Uke launches a sudden and unexpected punch Tori sidesteps and intercepts with his left while striking with an atemi to the hollow between the bicep and tricep insertion

He then steps behind Uke and throws his right arm around his neck

**And pulls
backward**

**Bringing Uke
down onto
his knee
(Be Careful!)**

Against an Unknown Form of Attack

Uke has convinced Tori beyond a reasonable doubt, with words and actions, that he means him harm

Before he gets a chance to move, Tori initiates his "attack defense" by kicking to the knee

Delivering a sword strike to the neck

And seizing the right wrist with his left hand

He locks it back back

And hyperextends it backwards. He then places his right hand under Uke's right elbow either pressing it upwards or striking it.

Against a "Sunday Punch"

Tori is menaced by Uke

As Uke attempts a swinging left punch, Tori deflects it with his right

Tori strikes Uke with an atemi to the neck

Tori gets behind Uke

Pressing him to the ground

and takes him to the ground by seizing his left wrist with his left and
applying a pressure point attack

Securing the lock

**And continuing the punishment
with a pressure point atemi**

Using Feints as "Fight Stoppers"

Tori and Uke face off

Tori has ascertained that Uke
intends to harm him

Tori feints a right

Uke instinctively attempts
to block the strike

Tori takes advantage of the opening to kick him in the rib cage or stomach

Tori then advances in and

Applies a twisting wrist lock

He now as the option of strike to the backor taking him to the ground

Against a Shove

Tori and Uke face off

As Uke attempts to push Tori

Tori grabs both arms and pulls him

Into a kick to the stomach

And takes him down with

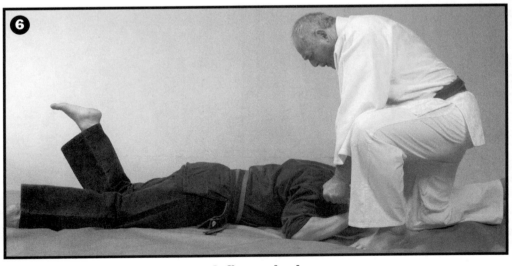

A finger lock

Against a Left Roundhouse Punch

Tori and Uke face off

Suddenly, Uke swings a left punch
toward Tori

Who blocks it

And seizes Uke's left wrist and
strikes with an atemi

Then steps around

And arm bars Uke over his shoulder

Pulling down on the arm and forcing Uke down

Against a Grab to the Head

Tori and Uke face off

Uke grabs Tori behind the head

And attempts to deliver a knee to the groin, which Tori parries

He then steps forward and grabs Uke's neck with his right hand

Steps behind trapping the arm

And brings him down

To the ground

**Where he finishes him with
a choke or pin**

Against a Headbutt

Uke and Tori face off

Uke tries to headbutt Tori

Who steps out of the way of the blow
and grabs him in a chin lock

He twists his hips, forcing Uke to the mat
Atemi strike to the upper chest

Where he steps around to apply an arm bar across the knee

Against a Side Kick

Uke menaces Tori

Uke attempts a low-line side kick and Tori steps out of the way

He then steps through and grabs Uke's head

Trapping his arm and stepping behind him

He wraps his left arm around Uke's free arm, trapping that as well

Then slips his right arm upTo apply a choke hold and hammer fist strike to the heart

Conclusion

I have never become bored with Jiu-Jitsu. My enthusiasm, interest and zeal for this art is still the same as when I first began to train more than fifty years ago. For me to walk on the mat is still an exciting experience. Throughout my martial arts career I have met and known many talented martial artists of various styles. The difference between them and me was that I never grew tired of training. I was always self-motivated. Others had more talent than I did. Others had more skill than I did, and others trained much harder than I.

"For me to walk on the mat is still an exciting experience."

However, most of these people quit the martial arts for one reason or another. Despite injuries and discouragement, despite the fact of the many obstacles that I had to face, I continued to train. I persevered with steadfast dedication and devotion that no one could extinquish. It was like an inner fire in my soul that could not be put out. I had to sacrifice and endure many hardships that are too personal and painful to mention in the book. Where did my motivation come from? Did it come from a particular martial art hero or heroes? No, it did not because I was wise enough to know that heroes have clay feet. Of course, I admired certain martial artists and I still do. I admire their talents and skills rather than their personalities, but my motivation came from within.

There are many different reasons that one studies the martial arts. Some study for self-defense, others for self-realization or physical fitness and enlightenment. Some study for a combination of all the reasons above. Do I believe that martial art masters are superior to other ordinary people? No, I do not believe this. There are some who are exceptional human beings. The ones who are exceptional are usually the non-commercial martial arts instructors.

In using this book try to train with a partner of equal height and weight. Train carefully and safely. Take one technique at a time and do it over and over again until you have mastered it or at least have a good working knowledge of it. Know how and why the techniques work. Read the instructions several times and study the photographs, Never forget that these techniques of combat Jiu-Jitsu are very effective. Several variations can be made from each technique. Remember you are only limited by your imagination.

These author does not claim that Jiu-Jitsu is better than any other martial art nor is it inferior. Each martial art has merits and flaws. There are certain martial arts that favor the young and the athletic. Other martial arts need a great deal of strength; however, all martial arts need a certain amount of strength and power in order to be effective. Some require more than others. Jiu-Jitsu has something for everyone. The young, the weak, the strong, and the aged can use Jiu-Jitsu techniques to overcome their adversaries.

At one time Jiu-Jitsu had over 700 different schools. Most schools were more similar than different. There are schools of Jiu-Jitsu that use very subtle techniques. There are schools that use very hard techniques. There are still others that use a combination of both soft and hard. Techniques of the hard schools of Jiu-Jitsu are used for a life and death struggle or on the battlefield. In the U.S.A. many of the urban city streets can be described as a battlefield therefore, there are times when one has to use savage fighting techniques to save one's life.

One never feels more alone in life than when one is faced with crazed adversary who wants to give you the beating of your life. I have been faced with this situation more than several times in my lifetime. It can be a feeling of sheer terror. Even though one shows self-composure, one can feel the reality of true fear. Thus, it becomes necessary for one to know some method of self-protection.

"Jiu–Jitsu has something for everyone."

Jiu-Jitsu is one such method that can turn this fear into a form of self-confidence. Bear in mind that these techniques have been used on the battlefields and for personal protection. If you do your part and train they will work for you too. The secret is to practice and train etc. This philosophy may save you and your loved ones from physical disaster one day.

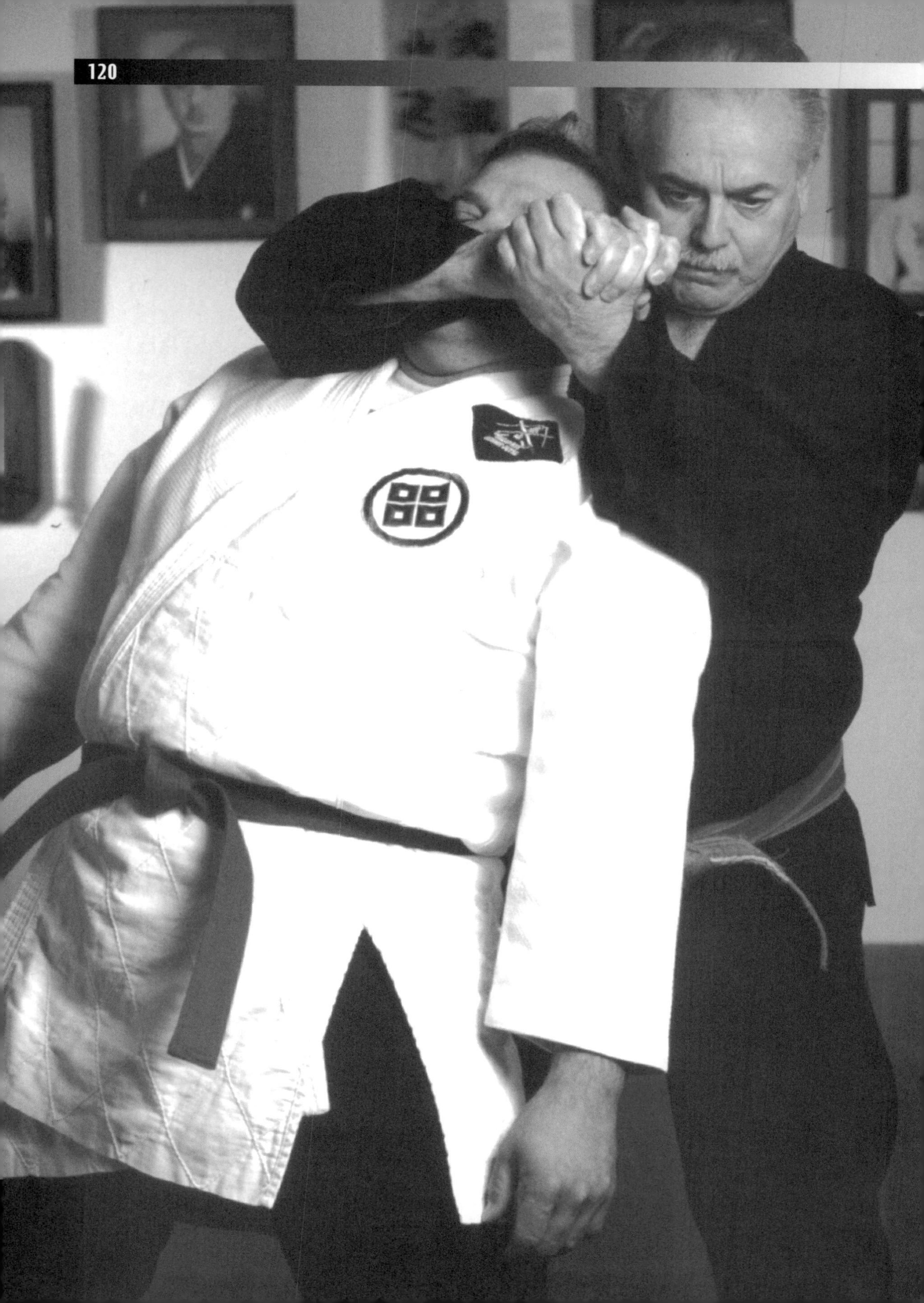

Epilogue

Remember, strategy is the most important factor in an encounter. A mediocre martial artist who is a good tactician will always win over a good martial artist who is a mediocre tactician. Of course, things happen awfully fast in a fight situation. Therefore, tactics must be drilled into the mind of the practitioner.

So in closing, if you don't take anything else away from reading this book, please memorize, practice and live by the following:

1. BASIC STRATEGY AND TACTICS.

If he pushes --------- you turn
If he pulls ----------- you enter
or
If he pushes -------- you pull
If he pulls ---------- you push

Techniques begin and end with atemi

Never oppose force with force. Always use your opponent's strength to defeat him. The atemi precedes all holds, projections and locks.

The art of body management is crucial in order to avoid getting hit and it will place the enemy in a very disadvantageous position. Know the vital spots of the human body the way you know the back of your hand.

For those of you who want to find out more about this martial art you may write to me at this address:

c/o C.F.W. ENTERPRISES, INC.
4201 VANOWEN PLACE
BURBANK, CALIF. 91505

Combat Jiu-Jitsu Videos

Featuring Norman Leff

Norman Leff started training as a teenager, more than 50 years ago and rapidly attained proficiency in several systems. While working in South America, Norman met a man named Kenji Tanaka. Tanaka, a former Japanese Imperial Marine, was well versed in the aspects of jiu-jitsu not conventionally taught to the public, even in Japan! For several years Norman trained under Tanaka Sensei, and today he holds the rank of headmaster in this rare and dynamic system of jiu-jitsu. Now, Norman Leff is ready to share over 50 years of knowledge and experience with you.

Volume 1
ATEMI WAZA STRIKING TECHNIQUES
Vital points, striking techniques and footwork.

CJJ01 – **$39.95**

Volume 2
LOCKS AND THROWS
Control techniques and jiu-jitsu's most effective throws.

CJJ02 – **$39.95**

Volume 3
COUNTERATTACK
When the other person makes the first move!

CJJ03 – **$39.95**

Volume 4
FIGHT STOPPERS
How to end a confrontation before it escalates.

CJJ014 – **$39.95**

All orders add $4.50 for ship. & Hand.
CA residents add 8.25% sales tax.

To Order Call:
1(800) 332-3330 • fax: 1(818) 845-7761
4201 Vanowen Place, Burbank, CA 91505

Notes

Notes

Notes

Martial Arts Titles

TITLE	BOOK #	PRICE
Action Kubotan Keychain	1100	$7.95
Advanced Balisong Manual, The	5192	$12.95
Advanced Iron Palm	416	$12.95
Aikido: Traditional and New Tomiki	319	$12.95
American Freestyle Karate	303	$9.95
Art of Stretching and Kicking, The	206	$7.95
Balisong Manual, The	5191	$12.95
Beginner's Tai Chi Chuan	280	$12.95
Beyond Kicking	421	$12.95
Bruce Lee's One & Three Inch Power Punch	502	$4.95
Bruce Lee: The Biography	144	$14.95
Bruce Lee: The Untold Story	401	$7.95
Chi Kung	240	$14.95
Chinese Healing Arts	222	$9.95
Chinese Kara-Ho Kempo, Volume 1	265	$16.95
Chinese Kara-Ho Kempo, Volume 2	266	$16.95
Choy Li Fut	217	$10.95
Complete Black Belt Hyung W.T.F., The	584	$15.95
Complete Guide to Kung-Fu Fighting Styles, The	221	$9.95
Complete Iron Palm	415	$12.95
Complete Martial Artist Vol. 1, The	5101	$19.95
Complete Martial Artist Vol. 2, The	5102	$19.95
Complete Master's Jumping Kick, The	581	$16.95
Complete Master's Kick, The	580	$16.95
Complete One and Three Step Sparring, The	582	$16.95
Complete Tae Geuk Hyung W.T.F., The	583	$15.95
Complete Tae Kwon Do Hyung Vol. 1, The	530	$13.95
Complete Tae Kwon Do Hyung Vol. 2, The	531	$13.95
Complete Tae Kwon Do Hyung Vol. 3, The	532	$13.95
Deadly Karate Blows	312	$10.95
Deceptive Hands of Wing Chun, The	201	$6.50
Dynamic Strength	209	$6.95
Dynamic Stretching and Kicking	405	$14.95
Effective Techniques of Unarmed Combat	130	$14.95
Effortless Combat Throws	261	$19.95
Enter The Dragon Deluxe Collector's Set	EDSP2	$49.98
Essence of Aikido, The	320	$10.95
Fatal Flute and Stick Form	215	$12.95
Fighting Weapons of Korean Martial Arts, The	355	$9.95
Filipino Fighting Arts: Theory and Practice	345	$19.95
Fundamentals of Pa Kua Chang, Vol. 1	245	$19.95
Fundamentals of Pa Kua Chang, Vol. 2	246	$24.95
Gene LeBell's Grappling World	593	$44.95

TITLE	BOOK #	PRICE
Hapkido: The Integrated Fighting Art	360	$12.95
Hsing-I	225	$14.95
Internal Secrets of Tai Chi Chuan	250	$12.95
Jackie Chan: The Best of Inside Kung-Fu	599	$12.95
Japanese Sword Drawing: A Sourcebook	114	$19.95
Jean Frenette's Complete Guide to Stretching	420	$10.95
Jeet Kune Do: A to Z, Volume	407	$14.95
Jeet Kune Do: A to Z, Volume 2	408	$16.95
Jeet Kune Do: Entering to Trapping to Grappling	403	$14.95
Jeet Kune Do: Its Concepts and Philosophies	410	$12.95
Jeet Kune Do Kickboxing	526	$14.95
Jeet Kune Do Vol. 2: Counter, Grapp. & Rev.	404	$12.95
Jeet Kune Do Unlimited	440	$14.95
Jo: The Japanese Short Staff	310	$12.95
Jun Fan Jeet Kune Do: The Textbook	528	$14.95
Kata and Kumite for Karate	558	$24.95
Kendo: The Way and Sport of the Sword	562	$17.95
Kenjustu: The Art of Japanese Swordsmanship	323	$12.95
Kokushi-ryu Jujutsu	322	$14.95
Koryu Aikido	321	$14.95
Kung-Fu: History, Philosophy, and Techniques	103	$14.95
Kung-Fu: The Endless Journey	230	$14.95
Kung-Fu: The Way of Life	202	$8.50
Making of Enter the Dragon, The	145	$13.95
Man of Contrasts	508	$16.95
Martial Arts Around the World	140	$12.95
Mas Oyama The Legend, The Legacy	317	$14.95
Ninjutsu History and Tradition	105	$12.95
Northern Sil Lum #7, Moi Fah	213	$8.95
Nunchaku: The Complete Guide	121	$12.95
Pai Lum Tao: Way of the White Dragon	257	$14.95
Pangu Mystical Qigong	242	$9.95
Practical Chin Na	260	$17.95
Science of Martial Arts Training, The	445	$19.95
Searching for the Way	180	$16.95
Secret History of the Sword, The	150	$19.95
Shaolin Chin Na	207	$10.95
Shaolin Fighting Theories and Concepts	205	$7.50
Shaolin Five Animals Kung-Fu	218	$9.95
Shaolin Long Fist Kung-Fu	208	$14.95
Study of Form Mind Boxing	235	$19.95
Super Karate for Kids	328	$10.95
Taekwondo Sparing: For the Ring & Street	356	$16.95

TITLE	BOOK #	PRICE
Tai Chi for Two: The Practice of Push Hands	568	$17.95
Tai Chi Sensing Hands	287	$19.95
Tai Chi Thirteen Sword	285	$19.95
Tai Chi Training in China	567	$25.00
Taijutsu: Ninja Art of Unarmed Combat	125	$12.95
Tang Soo Do	585	$16.95
Tao of Health & Fitness	270	$12.95
Tomiki Aikido: Randori & Koryu No Kat	551	$17.95
Total Quality Martial Arts	447	$16.95
Traditional Ninja Weapons	108	$9.50
Training and Fighting Skills	402	$14.95
Ultimate Kick, The	406	$12.95
Warrior Walking	155	$14.95
Warrior Within	450	$14.95
Wing Chun Bil Jee	214	$10.95
Wu Style of Tai Chi Chuan, The	211	$9.95
Xing Yi Nei Gong	226	$19.95
Yang Style Tai Chi Chuan	210	$14.50
Yuen Kay-San Wing Chun Kuen	275-1	$16.95

ᑌᑭ

Unique Publications

4201 W. Vanowen Place
Burbank, CA 91505
Phone: (818) 845-2656 • Fax: (818) 845-7761

www.cfwenterprises.com